Haunted Britain

Jane Rollason

LEVEL 1

SCHOLASTIC

Material written by: Jane Rollason
Commissioning Editor: Jacquie Bloese
Editor: Fiona Beddall
Cover design: Ian Butterworth, Emily Spencer
Designer: Dawn Wilson
Illustrators: Paul Davies, Steve Lillie
Picture research: Emma Bree
Photo credits: Cover: Photodisc Green/Getty Images.
Pages 4 & 5: Imagesource; Stockbyte; Hemera;
L. Petro/Alamy. **Page 20:** R. Anania/Fog Stock/Alamy.
Pages 22 & 23: N. McDiarmid/Alamy; Pixtal/Powerstock;
I. Addicoat/www.ghosthunting.org.uk.
Page 25: I. Britton/Freefoto.com. **Page 27:** A. Muttutt/Alamy.

The publishers would like to acknowledge the following teachers for reporting on the manuscript:

Carine Chaput, Collège Ozar Hatorah, Toulouse, France

Kleio Drosou, Vytina High School, Arcadia, Greece

Beata Eigner, GRG, Vienna, Austria

Marie-Christine Jacquot, Collège Saint-Maimboeuf, Montbeliard, France

Adele James, Nea Paideia, Hydrari, Greece

Brigitte Neustifter, SHS Weiz, Weiz, Austria

Gertraud Noeth, Christian-von-Bomhard Schule, Uffenheim, Germany

Theodora Papavasiliou, English Language Centre, Trikala, Greece

Monique Peubez, Institution des Chartreux, Lyon, France

Maria Santoliquido, IPSCP 'Marcello Dudovich', Milan, Italy

No part of this publication may be reproduced in whole or in part, or stored in a retrieval system, or transmitted in any form or by any means, electronic, mechanical, photocopying, recording or otherwise, without written permission of the publisher. For information regarding permission write to:

Mary Glasgow Magazines (Scholastic Inc.)
Commonwealth House
1–19 New Oxford Street
London WC1A 1NU

© Mary Glasgow Magazines,
an imprint of Scholastic Inc. 2005
All rights reserved.

Printed in Italy.

CONTENTS

THE GHOST OF TILLY TURNER

TILLY TURNER

JAZMINDA

How old: 14
Lives: two streets from Josh, with her mother, father and two sisters
School: Year 10, St Margaret's, Highgate
Favourite band: Outkast
Likes: the cinema, the Waterlow Club, playing tennis
Best friends: lots
Boyfriend: Josh

JOSH

How old: 14
Lives: No.63 Flask Road in Highgate, London, with his mother and grandmother
School: Year 10, St Margaret's, Highgate
Favourite band: Red Hot Chili Peppers
Likes: the Waterlow Club, playing football, playing the guitar
Best friend: Flynn
Girlfriend: Jazminda

PLACES

St Margaret's School, Highgate: A school for boys and girls from 11 to 16 years old.

Waterlow Club, Highgate: A place for teenagers in the evenings. They can dance, DJ, watch MTV and talk.

Highgate Cemetery: A very big London cemetery. It opened in 1839. There are a lot of famous graves here.

THE GHOST OF

Chapter 1 BOOM!

Josh was in bed. Suddenly … BOOM! His pictures blew off the walls. The door blew open. There were bits of window on his bed and on the floor. And there was dust – lots and lots of it.

'I can't see! Mum! Gran!' he shouted. He ran out of his room. 'Where are you? Are you OK?'

Josh's grandmother was still in bed. He helped her and together they went out of the house. His mum was already in the street.

The house next to theirs – No.65 – wasn't there! Well, it was still there … but it wasn't a house now. There was just a front wall and a lot of bricks. Josh and his family waited and watched. The people from the other houses in the street were there too. Suddenly the front wall came down. There were more bricks and dust in the street. Everyone shouted. There was a cold wind on Josh's face. It blew out of the bricks.

TILLY TURNER

'What was that?' asked Josh. But no one answered. Josh arrived at school at 8.45. He met his girlfriend Jaz in the classroom and told her about No.65.

'No! I don't believe it!' she said. 'Was anyone in the house?'

'No. They're on holiday in Egypt. They didn't turn off the gas in the kitchen, so there was a lot of gas in the house. Then something turned on … a light or something … and BOOM! The police think …'

But Josh didn't finish. There was a face … a girl … next to the door. Suddenly he was cold.

'Who …?' he whispered. Everything was quiet. There was only her face. She was older than him and pretty. But she wasn't happy.

He looked at Jaz. Then he looked across the room again. But where was the girl? She wasn't there.

Something touched his arm.

'What?!' He turned quickly.

'What's up, Josh?' asked Jaz. 'What are you looking at?'

'There was a girl … near the door,' he said. 'Who was she?'

'What girl?' asked Jaz. Josh didn't answer. 'I didn't see anyone. Are you feeling OK?'

'Yeah. I'm cool,' he said. He tried to forget about that face.

Chapter 2 Tilly Turner

Jaz came to Josh's house that evening.

'There's a lot of dust!' she said.

'The gas people came,' said Josh's mum. 'They cleaned the house, but it's still dirty.'

'Well, we're luckier than the people at No.65,' said Gran.

Josh ran down from his room. 'Hi,' he called to Jaz. Then he saw her. 'Hey! You look … fantastic,' he said and smiled. 'Bye, Mum. Bye, Gran,' he called.

'Be home before 11,' shouted his mum.

They stopped at No.65. Jaz wanted to see it.

They looked at the sad, dark place. A wind started to blow.

'Let's go to the club,' Josh said quickly. 'I don't like it here.'

Together they ran down the road.

'What do you want to drink?' Josh asked Jaz at the Waterlow Club.

'Just water for me, please,' said Jaz. 'Oh, look! There's Em. I must talk to her.'

'OK,' said Josh. He ordered the drinks. There was a DJ tonight – someone from their school – and there were a lot of people in the club. Josh waited for the drinks. His friend Flynn was there. They talked about football. And then, across the room, he saw that face again.

'Hey, Flynn. Who's that girl?'

'What girl?'

'Look! She's standing next to Jaz. She's got long brown hair and she's wearing a blue shirt and a white skirt. Her clothes are funny… I don't know, from the 1950s or something. She's looking at us.'

'I can't see anyone,' Flynn laughed. 'Did a brick from

No.65 fall on your head this morning? Something isn't right …'

'She *is* there! It's that girl from school. I saw her this morning. Who is she?' He looked at Flynn. But Flynn just laughed again.

They gave Jaz her drink and then watched Outkast on MTV. Well, Jaz and Flynn watched.

'This music is fantastic,' Jaz said to Josh. 'I'm going to buy the new Outkast CD tomorrow. Do you want to come and listen to it at my house?' But Josh didn't answer. 'Are you listening to me? What are you looking at?' She was angry. 'What's up with you today?'

'It's that girl … from this morning. What's she doing here?' said Josh.

'What girl?!' shouted Jaz.

'Look – there. She's standing next to the door.'

'THERE'S NO ONE THERE, JOSH!' Jaz walked away angrily.

Josh didn't move. 'Flynn can't see her. Jaz can't see her. How can I see her?' he thought. He was frightened.

The girl was still there. She looked at him and then she walked out of the club. He didn't want to go with her; he wanted to stay at the club. But he followed her anyway.

She waited for him in the street, near the club door. She didn't have a coat.

'Are you cold?' Josh asked. He was cold, too, very cold, but he gave her his jacket. 'Let's go. I'm going to walk home with you,' he said. 'Where do you live?'

She didn't answer. She turned and walked across the road. Josh followed.

'I don't know your name,' said Josh.

'Tilly. Tilly Turner.' Did she speak? Or did the wind whisper the words?

She stopped at the cemetery.

'We can't go in there,' Josh said. 'They close the gate at night.'

She pointed at the gate and, very slowly, it opened.

Chapter 3 The cemetery at night

Tilly went into the cemetery and waited. Josh didn't want to go through the gate. 'But I can't leave Tilly,' he thought. Then he said loudly, 'I'm going first.'

Tilly pointed to a small path.

'I often come in here,' said Josh. 'But not at night. It's different in the dark …'

It started to rain. They walked next to the graves. Suddenly, something ran across Josh's foot.

'What was that?'

Something touched his face.

'YEUCH! That's wet!'

He turned to Tilly. She was behind him.

'You don't say much. What's up?' he said. He laughed, but he was frightened. Why didn't she talk to him?

Tilly pointed to a little path on the right. Wet trees touched their faces. It was very dark. Josh stopped and listened. There were whispers. Who was it? Was it the dead people?

The path stopped. 'Where now?' Josh asked.

Tilly pointed through the trees.

'Why are we going this way?' But Tilly just looked at him with her sad green eyes.

They started to walk again. 'We can't go through here,' Josh said. 'There are too many trees.' He put his arms in front of his face. 'I can't see,' he called.

Suddenly his foot touched something hard.

'OW!' he shouted. There was a gravestone at his feet.

'Are you OK?' he called to Tilly. But she didn't answer. She wasn't there.

He went back but he didn't find her. Where was she?

'Tilly! Tilly!' he called, louder and louder. 'WHERE ARE YOU?'

He ran. 'I can't see the path!' Josh thought. He ran into a gravestone and cut his nose. 'YEOW!' he shouted.

Then he found a path. But where was Tilly? He called her name, again and again.

'I'm never going to find the gate,' he thought.

He walked for a long time in the dark and the rain. 'They're going to find my dead body in here in the morning.' He was very wet now, and his T-shirt and jeans were very dirty. But then he saw it. The gate!

He ran. But the gate started to close.

'NOOOOO!' he shouted.

He ran faster. He ran through the gate and – BANG! – it closed just behind him.

Chapter 4 'I don't believe in ghosts!'

The next day was Saturday – no school. Josh got up late. 'What's wrong with me?' he thought. 'Why did I leave a girl in a cemetery … alone … in the dark?

He dressed and had some coffee. He didn't want any breakfast. 'I must find her,' he thought.

The cemetery was open. It was a nice day and there were a lot of people there. They wanted to see the famous gravestones. But Josh thought about the night before.

'I didn't want to follow Tilly. Why did I go with her? Is she a …? No! Of course she isn't a ghost. I don't believe in ghosts.'

He walked faster. 'But only I can see her,' he thought. 'Jaz and Flynn can't see her.' He was cold … cold and frightened.

He looked for the path from the night before. He walked from one end of the cemetery to the other, but he didn't find it. 'OK. I'm going home,' he decided.

Suddenly he saw something through the trees. It was red. What was it? He followed the path and then he found it. His jacket! His red jacket! It was on a gravestone.

He was happier now. 'Tilly put it there for me,' he thought. 'She was OK last night. She knew the way out of the cemetery.' He took the jacket and turned back. But a cold wind blew across his face. 'Look! Look!' the wind whispered in his ear. He looked at the gravestone. 'Edward Turner. 1926–1973.'

'Turner?' he said quietly. 'Tilly Turner? Edward Turner?'

Josh went home. His grandmother was in the kitchen.
'Your face is white, Josh! Is something wrong?'

He told her everything. 'I was very frightened, Gran.'

'Well!' she said. She gave him some tea. 'I can
understand some of it. I was at school with Tilly. We were
friends. We finished school at 14 and went out to work.
And then she met a man – Edward Turner. Ed, she called
him. No one liked him, but she didn't listen to us. She
married him and they moved to the house next to ours –
No.65. Ed was older than Tilly, maybe 30. She was only 16.
I saw her most days after work. Then I didn't see her for
three or four weeks. She didn't answer the door. One day
my mum said, "You know that Tilly Turner? You're not
going to see her again. She met a younger man and left.
There's only Ed at No.65 now." "Good," I thought. "Tilly's
going to be happier without her husband."'

Josh said nothing at first. 'She *is* a ghost, then,' he said
after some minutes. He didn't like the idea. 'But why can I
see her? What does she want from me?'

'Some people *can* see ghosts,' said his grandmother.
'Only a few people. You're very special, Josh.'

Josh got up from the table. He didn't want to hear this.
'I'm not special,' he shouted. 'AND I DON'T BELIEVE IN
GHOSTS!'

He went out in the afternoon. 'I must talk to Jaz,' he

thought. 'She's going to be very angry with me.' He phoned her mobile but she didn't answer. He stopped at No.65 and looked at the bricks. And then he saw … what was it? … a door? … something under the bricks. 'I didn't see that last time,' he thought. A cold wind started to blow. Old cans and chocolate papers danced down the street. He put his hands over his ears.

'No! NO!' he shouted. 'I CAN'T HELP YOU!'

He turned and ran.

Chapter 5 The room under the house

Josh closed his eyes. He ran down the street … and into Jaz. He was right. She *was* very angry.

'Josh! I do NOT want to talk to you.' Josh didn't answer. 'Where did you go last night? Why did you go without me? Never –' She stopped.

Josh's face was white. She looked at his frightened eyes and touched him. He was cold, very cold.

'Josh, what's up?' She took his arm. 'Josh?' She was sorry now. 'Let's go and have a coffee.'

They walked slowly to a café. They sat at a table near the window and talked for hours.

'It can't be true,' Jaz said. But when she looked at Josh's face … into his eyes … she knew. It was true.

'What does Tilly want?' asked Josh.

'Let's go and look at No.65,' said Jaz. 'Maybe the answer's there.'

It was evening now. They went to Josh's house first and found a torch. Then they climbed over the fence to No.65. The wind started again.

They moved some bricks away and found a door there. Josh pulled the door.

'I can't open it,' he said.

'Let's try together,' said Jaz. They pulled hard … harder. Suddenly it opened – BANG! They pointed the torch through the door. There was a room – a room under the house.

Josh went down first. He took Jaz's hand.

'Are you OK?' he asked her.

'Yeah, yeah. I'm cool,' she said. But she didn't feel cool. She was frightened.

There was no sound. The room was wet and cold and dirty. Josh pointed into the dark with his torch. Suddenly they saw a long box near the wall.

'AAAHHH! Wh-What's that?' asked Jaz. 'I can't do this, Josh. Let's go.'

'No. Wait a minute,' he said.

'But I'm frightened.'

'Me too. Just a minute.' Josh went nearer. 'Take the torch. Point it at the box.' He pulled the top of the box and it came away in his hands. There was lots of dust.

'WHOAH!' shouted Jaz and Josh. They looked through the dust. Two black eyes looked back at them.

'A skeleton!' whispered Jaz. 'There's a skeleton in the box!'

'And look,' said Josh. 'It's wearing a blue shirt and a white skirt …'

Suddenly, some bricks moved behind them. They turned and looked at the door.

'It's closing,' shouted Josh. Jaz got out first and pulled Josh behind her. But the door came down on his head.

'OW!' he cried. Someone laughed.

'Who was that?' asked Josh from behind the door.

'Are you OK?' called Jaz. She pulled on the door and opened it again.

'No, I'm not OK. I don't like this place,' he said.

They quickly ran to the fence. A cold wind blew around them. 'It's a ghost,' Josh said. 'I can feel it. Tilly? Tilly? Is that you?'

But it wasn't Tilly. He knew that. This was a bad ghost. 'Quickly, Jaz. Let's go – NOW.'

They climbed over the fence and into the street. The wind was louder now. They ran to No.63. The wind followed. Something was there, just behind them. Josh pulled Jaz into the house with him. He closed the door, hard, and took Jaz's hand. They didn't make a sound. They listened and waited. Slowly, very slowly, the sound of the wind went away. They were safe.

Chapter 6 The ghost can leave

In the morning, Josh phoned the police. They came and put a bigger fence around No.65. At 3 o'clock the skeleton came out. There were lots of TV and newspaper people in the street. They talked to Josh's grandmother. They wanted to talk to Josh and Jaz, but Josh and Jaz didn't come out.

A policewoman came to No.63 in the afternoon.

'We found her,' she said. 'You were right, Josh – it *is* Tilly Turner. And we found something interesting next to her skeleton.' She gave him a photo.

'What is it?' asked Jaz.

'It's a penknife,' answered Josh. 'Look.'

'It's got letters on it – E T,' said Jaz.

'E T? Edward Turner!' shouted Josh's grandmother. 'I knew it! Tilly didn't meet a younger man – Ed killed her!' She put her hands over her face.

Josh took her hand. 'It's OK, Gran. It was a long time ago. Tilly's happy now. She wanted to tell us about Ed. Now we know about him, so her ghost can leave No.65.'

'Her ghost?' said the policewoman.

Josh looked at Gran. He smiled. She smiled too.

A week after this, Josh, Jaz and their families were in Highgate Cemetery next to Tilly's family grave. Tilly's brothers were there. They were old now and very sad about Tilly. The TV and newspaper people were there too.

Tilly's skeleton went into the family grave, with her father and mother. Josh remembered that night in the cemetery. He was happier now, because it wasn't dark. Then he saw something blue behind the TV cameras. Was it … ? Yes, it was Tilly's shirt! Tilly was there. But not the old, sad Tilly. She wasn't sad now – she was happy. She smiled at him. He took Jaz's hand and then looked for Tilly again. But Tilly wasn't there. 'Good. She's OK now. Maybe I'm going to be OK too,' he thought.

It was a hot day. Josh and Jaz walked to the gate. The newspaper men followed them.

'Just one more picture,' they called. Josh and Jaz smiled for the cameras.

Then Josh saw a face, near the gate. The face looked at him. It was a boy – a young boy. Suddenly everything was quiet. Josh didn't hear the people or the cameras. And he was very cold.

'What's up, Josh?' asked Jaz. 'What are you looking at now?!'

URBAN

THE QUEENSWAY GHOST

One of the biggest roads into the city of Liverpool in England is Queensway. About 20 years ago, a man on a motorbike was on this road. He saw a hitch-hiker by the road. The hitch-hiker was a boy, about 18 years old. The man stopped for him. There were a lot of cars and they went slowly down the road. The man and the boy had a conversation.

'Where do you live?' asked the man.

'Not far from here. Next to the Black Cat pub in Southport,' said the boy.

After a few minutes, the man turned to the boy again. But he wasn't there! Where was he? The man looked and looked but he didn't find him.

A few days after this, the man was in Southport. He went to the boy's house. A woman answered the door. He told her about the boy.

'That's my son,' she said. 'Five years ago, he was on his motorbike on Queensway. A car drove into him and he died.'

Find these words in the pictures: motorbike   hitch-hiker

MYTHS

THE HOOK

In London in the 1960s, Gill had a boyfriend. His name was Tom. In the 1960s there weren't many interesting places for teenagers in the evenings. One Friday night, Tom and Gill drove to Crystal Palace Park. It was dark and quiet. Tom turned on the radio. Then he put his arm around Gill.

'This is a police message,' said the radio. 'Police in Crystal Palace are looking for a man with a hook in place of his right arm. Do not go near him. It isn't safe.'

'Tom! We must leave here,' said Gill.

'He's not going to come into the park,' said Tom. 'Everything's OK.' He put his other arm around Gill.

'Please, Tom! Let's go,' said Gill.

Tom was angry. He didn't want to go. He started the car and drove quickly back to Gill 's house. He got out and walked around the car. He wanted to open Gill 's car door for her.

'AAAHHHH!!!' he shouted.

Gill got out of the car.

There, on her car door, was … a hook.

> Do you think these stories are true? Do you know any good stories about cities in your country?

Find this word in the picture: hook

Creepy castles

Let's hear from the ghosts...

'They call me the Blue Boy. I cry every night at 12 o'clock.
People hear me and feel cold.

They found my skeleton in 1920 in the wall of the castle. My father
hated me. He put me in the wall. He didn't give me any food or
water. My mother called my name day and night. I shouted to her,
but she didn't hear me. After three weeks, I died ... at 12 o'clock.
That was in 1665. Sometimes I come out of the wall and stand by
the bed. My clothes are blue.'

Chillingham Castle, Northumberland

'**My name's Ella** and I'm 13 years old. I love dancing. I dance all day and all night. One night, about 300 years ago, I danced at the top of the tallest tower in the castle. A wind started suddenly and blew me off the tower. I died. Lots of people come to see the castle now. Sometimes I ask them, 'Do you want to dance with me?' But no one says yes. It makes me sad.'

Pengersick Castle, Cornwall

I'm Mary, Queen of Scots. In 1567 I married my third husband in this castle. But that night, some men came here. They wanted to kill me. I dressed in boy's clothes and left the castle. Luckily, no one saw me. But in 1587 my cousin, Queen Elizabeth I of England, wanted me dead. Her men cut off my head. I still haunt a lot of Scottish castles. At Borthwick I always wear boy's clothes.

Borthwick Castle, Scotland

Work with a friend. One of you is a castle ghost. The other is staying at the castle. Have a conversation.

Find these words in the pictures: castle tower

Cornwall:
land of legend

Cornwall is famous for its empty country and sea storms – and for its stories and ghosts.

King Arthur

King Arthur was a British king around 500 AD*. There are a lot of books and films about him, but no one knows the true story. In most of the stories, Arthur came from Cornwall. Tintagel Castle was his first home. The ghost of Merlin the Magician still lives near the castle.

*AD: years after Jesus Christ

The spirits of the mine

Long ago, spirits lived and worked in the mines of Cornwall. Then people found the mines and started to work in them. But the spirit miners didn't go away.

Tom Trevorrow was a miner at St Just. He was never happy. One day he heard the spirit miners.

'Go away,' he shouted at them. 'Leave us some cake, Tom Trevorrow,' they answered, 'or bad things are going to happen to you.'

Tom had some cake in his lunch bag. But Tom wasn't very clever. He decided to eat it all. He didn't leave any cake for the spirits.

The next day, the walls of his mine came down. Then water came into the mine. It wasn't possible to work there. Tom closed his mine and bought some fields.

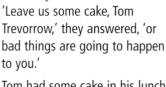

> What other bad things happened to Tom Trevorrow, do you think?

Find these words in the picture: spirit mine miner

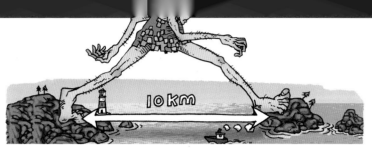

10 km

Bolster the giant

Once Cornwall was the home of giants. They had a big castle at Trecobben. They took people to their castle and had them for dinner.

One giant's name was Bolster. Bolster loved Agnes and he followed her all the time. She was angry with him. 'You have a wife and I do not love you. Do not speak to me again.' But he didn't listen.

'Right,' she said. 'I'm going to test your love for me. Put your blood into this hole. I want to see blood all the way to the top.' The giant cut his arm. His blood ran into the hole. 'This isn't going to take long,' he thought. But the hole stayed empty. All the giant's blood ran into the hole and he died. Why did the hole stay empty? Because it went down into the sea below. You can still see the hole today at Chapel Porth. Everything around the hole is red from the giant's blood.

Chapel Porth

Look at Bolster. How tall is he?

Find these words in the pictures: giant blood hole sea

25

BLACK SHUCK:

It's cold and dark. It's raining. The wind is blowing. You're walking home on a quiet path.

Suddenly you hear feet behind you. Not the feet of a man – these are animal feet. The feet are louder now. You look around and see something black. It's moving.

It's coming nearer and nearer. It's a big black dog – Black Shuck! Quick! Close your eyes! Don't look into Black Shuck's red eyes, or someone in your family is going to die before the end of the year!

Arthur Conan Doyle got the idea for his famous Sherlock Holmes story, *The Hound of the Baskervilles*, from Black Shuck. The stories about Black Shuck come from East Anglia in England. The land here is flat, wet and empty. People often see Black Shuck. Sometimes Black Shuck has no head or only one big eye.

dog of the dead ✷

East Anglia

Here's one story about
Black Shuck.

Bungay is a small town in East Anglia. One Sunday morning in 1577, the people of Bungay were in church. There was a big storm and the sky was dark. Suddenly Black Shuck ran through the church.

There were two people at the front of the church. The dog ran between them and they were dead. The dog then ran into a third man. Suddenly a fire started around him. He died too. At the same minute, the same thing happened in Blythburgh, 10 kilometres away. A black dog ran into the church. It killed three people and ran away. Parts of the church door were black from fire. The door is still like that today.

There are stories about black dogs in many parts of Britain. Do you know any animal stories like this from your country?

Bungay Church

Find these words in the pictures: animal church

A GHOST-HUNTER'S GUIDE

Do you want to see a ghost?
Use these ideas and ... who knows?

1 Don't go alone!
Go with some good friends.

2 Choose a haunted place.

a castle

an old house

an old train station

a pub

3 Don't forget to tell your parents.

4 Take these things.

talcum powder

a pen and paper

a microphone and tape recorder

a video camera

chocolate

a mobile

trainers

a torch

your dog

Work with three friends. You looked for ghosts last night.
What happened? Talk about it. Then tell the class.

Chapters 1-2

Before you read

1 Match the verbs with their definitions.

blow   whisper   follow   touch   fall

   a) say words very quietly
   b) put your hand on something
   c) go from a high place to the floor by mistake
   d) walk behind someone
   e) the wind does this

2 Complete the sentences with these words. Use your dictionary to help you.

bricks   cemetery   dust   fence   gas   gate   ghost

   a) The ... walked through the wall.
   b) We cook our food with ... .
   c) All the dead people in his family are in the same ... .
   d) There are big dogs behind this ... . Don't open the ... or they can get out!
   e) We didn't want a wall here, so we pulled down the ... . There was a lot of ... all through the house.

After you read

3 Are these sentences true or false? Correct the false sentences.

   a) The front wall of Josh's house falls down.
   b) A cold wind blows out of the bricks of No.65.
   c) The people from No.65 are not at home.
   d) In the classroom, Jaz can see the girl near the door.
   e) Jaz spends the evening at Josh's house.
   f) Jaz is angry with Josh because he doesn't like Outkast.

4 What do you think?

   a) Is Josh going to follow Tilly into the cemetery?
   b) Who is Tilly?
   c) What's going to happen in the cemetery?

Chapters 3-4

Before you read

5 Choose the best sentence.

   a) **i** You can't run on a path.

       ii You can drive a car on a path.

      iii You can walk on a path.

   b) **i** A big stone dropped on her head and killed her.

       ii A cat walked over her foot and killed her.

      iii Someone called on her mobile and killed her.

   c) **i** I like you and I want to marry you.

       ii I hate you and I want to marry you.

      iii I love you and I want to marry you.

   d) **i** She's wet because of the rain.

       ii She's wet because she likes going to the cinema.

      iii She's wet because she has nice clothes.

   e) **i** He cut the cake with some coffee.

       ii He cut the cake into five bits.

      iii He cut the cake because no one liked it.

6 Is there a famous cemetery in your city/town? Who is in it?

7 In Chapter 4, Josh finds a gravestone. What name is on it? Write your ideas.

After you read

8 Answer the questions.

   a) Why does Josh leave the cemetery without Tilly?

   b) Josh sees his red jacket on the gravestone. Why does he feel better then?

   c) What did Gran's mother tell her about Tilly?

   d) Why is Josh special?

   e) Why does he want to talk to Jaz?

9 What do you think?

   a) Why doesn't Tilly speak?

   b) Why does Tilly go down the small paths in the cemetery?

   c) What is there going to be under the bricks at No.65?

Chapters 5-6

Before you read

10 Match the two columns.

   a) A hundred years after a person is dead, there is only a ...
   b) You can cut things with a ...
   c) You can see in the dark with a ...
   d) New shoes usually come in a ...

   i torch.
   ii box.
   iii skeleton.
   iv penknife.

11 Is Josh still going to be Jaz's boyfriend at the end of the story?

After you read

12 Josh meets Jaz in the street. Answer the questions.
   a) Why does Jaz feel sorry?
   b) Does she believe Josh's story?
   c) Does she want to help him?

13 True or false?
   a) There's a room under the house.
   b) They find Ed Turner in a box.
   c) Jaz laughs because the door falls on Josh's head.
   d) Tilly's ghost follows them to Josh's house.
   e) Ed killed Tilly with his penknife.
   f) Ed put Tilly in a box in the room under the house.
   g) Josh's grandmother knew about Tilly's skeleton under the house.
   h) Tilly's ghost is still not happy.
   i) Josh sees Ed's ghost at the cemetery.

14 What do you think?
   a) Is Jaz a good girlfriend for Josh? Why/Why not?
   b) Josh is special because he can see ghosts. Is this a good thing or a bad thing? Why?